13.95

W9-BIS-525

·THE·WAY·IT·WORKS·

Water

PHILIP SAUVAIN

new
Discovery
B·O·O·K·S
NEW YORK

First American publication 1992 by New Discovery Books, Macmillan Publishing Company, 866 Third Avenue, New York, NY 10022

Macmillan Publishing Company is part of the Maxwell Communication Group of Companies

First published in 1991 by
Heinemann Children's Reference,
a division of Heinemann Educational Books Ltd,
Halley Court, Jordan Hill, Oxford OX2 8EJ

Library of Congress Cataloging in Publication Data
Sauvain, Philip Arthur
    Water / by Philip Sauvain
      p. cm. – – The Way It Works
    Includes index.
    Summary: Discusses the properties, uses, and changing nature of water.
    ISBN 0-02-781078-X
    1. Water -- Juvenile literature. (1. Water) I. Title.
    II. Series:
    GB662.3.S28   1992
    553.7--dc20   91-119145

Photographic credits
t = top b = bottom r = right l = left

Cover NHPA; 5*t* NHPA; 5*b* Planet Earth; 2 ZEFA; 9*br* Planet Earth; 14 Nordic Saunas; 15*b* Aquatech; 16 Mansell Collection; 18 Water Board; 21*tr* Mansell Collection; 22*tr*, 22*bl*, 24*bl*, 27*t* Trevor Hill; 29*tr* Philip Sauvain; 29*c* Colorific; 29*br* ZEFA; 32 Philip Sauvain; 33*br* Images of India; 34*t* Planet Earth; 35*tr* Trevor Hill; 37*bl*, 38 Planet Earth; 40 Robert Harding; 43 Science Photo Library

Designed and produced by Pardoe Blacker Limited, Lingfield, Surrey, England
Artwork by Terry Burton, Tony Gibbons, Jane Pickering, Sebastian Quigley, Craig Warwick and Brian Watson

Printed in Spain by Mateu Cromo

91 92 93 94 95 10 9 8 7 6 5 4 3 2 1

Note to the reader

In this book there are some words in the text which are printed in **bold** type. This shows that the word is listed in the glossary on page 46. The glossary gives a brief explanation of words which may be new to you.

Contents

The changing nature of water

All living things need water. Without water all human life, animal life, and plant life dies. Some animals and plants have ways of storing water for use when the weather is dry. Many of them live in hot, dry areas of the world. Other living things may spend all their time in the sea or in fresh water.

The same but different

Water is the only thing on the Earth which you can find in nature in three different forms. You can see this at home. When you take an ice cube from the refrigerator, it is **solid** water. If you put it in a pan and warm it, the ice melts into **liquid** water. If you heat the water, hot steam will rise from the pan. This is water as a **gas**.

Water boils at a **temperature** of 212°F (100°C). This is called the **boiling point** of water. It freezes into solid ice at a temperature of 32°F (0°C). This is called its **freezing point**.

How water behaves

Many things can be squeezed into a smaller space. A large sheet of aluminum foil can be crumpled into a ball. You cannot squeeze liquid water into a smaller space. No matter how hard you try, liquid water always stays the same size. Squashing a hot water bottle only makes it burst.

Some things float in water, while others sink. Many **crystals**, such as salt and sugar, disappear when they are stirred in water. They mix with the water to make a **solution**. But the tiny crystals of salt or sugar are still there, even though you can see right through the water.

Moving water can also be very powerful. You can see this when you watch the waves crash against the beach. We use the power of moving water to make many things work for us. We say moving water is a source of **energy**.

ice – below 32°F (0°C)

water –32°–211°F (1°–99°C)

gas – above 212°F (100°C)

The three forms of water
It is sometimes difficult to believe that water is a **molecule** made of two gases: **hydrogen** and **oxygen**.

▲ This place is a desert. For a few days after it has rained, thousands of plants grow and flower. Their life cycle is short. Without the rain they would have no life at all.

Using water

Water has many different uses. Sometimes we use it to cool things. We run it through a car engine, or spray it on a tooth as it is drilled. Sometimes we use it to heat things, such as fish cooked in steam or a room heated by a radiator. Boats and ships use water as a means of transportation. This book will tell you about some of the machines and household appliances that use water and how they work.

▲ These plants are able to store water in their fleshy leaves and stems. They are called succulents. Cacti store water in their stems and live in very dry climates. Leaf succulents store water in their leaves and grow in damper conditions.

5

How your body uses water

About 60 percent of your body is water! You can tell this from a number of clues. A lot of water comes out of your body each day in the form of waste. This includes the things in your blood that your body doesn't need and that could make you ill. Water also comes out of your skin as sweat when you get hot. Water comes out of your eyes too, when you cry. We use and get rid of water in many ways every day. The amount we use varies. It depends on the weather, what we do, eat, and drink.

Waste products

Getting rid of waste is one of the main ways in which your body uses water. You use a part of your body called the **kidneys** to do this. The kidneys clean the blood by taking out any substances that could be harmful. These are mixed with water to make a liquid called urine. The urine travels down tubes called the **ureters** to be stored in the bladder. The bladder is a small bag like a balloon. When the bladder is full, messages are sent to the brain to say that the bladder needs emptying. When we go to the toilet the urine passes out of the bladder through a tube called the **urethra**.

Eating and drinking

You replace the water you get rid of during the day when you drink and when you eat. Most drinks, even milk, contain a large amount of water. Most foods, such as meat, vegetables, fruit, and bread, also contain lots of water. This is why they shrivel up when they dry out. Your skin would dry up, too, if you cut down the amount of water you drank. You would also lose weight. You would become **dehydrated** as you lose water.

Tears in your eyes

When you cry, water comes out of your tear ducts. If you get dust or an eyelash in your eye, your eyes "water". The body uses water to protect the delicate parts of your eye from damage. Like sweat, your tears are slightly salty.

Your body

When you do a lot of exercise, or get too hot, your body sweats. When you sweat you lose a lot of water. The water comes out of holes in your skin called **pores**. Sweating cools you down. The water takes heat away from your body and releases it into the air (like steam). If you could collect the water you lose when you sweat, you might be able to fill a quart bottle in about half an hour!

The liquid in your nose is called **mucus**. It protects the lining of your nose.

Liquid in your mouth helps you to eat and digest food. This is called **saliva**.

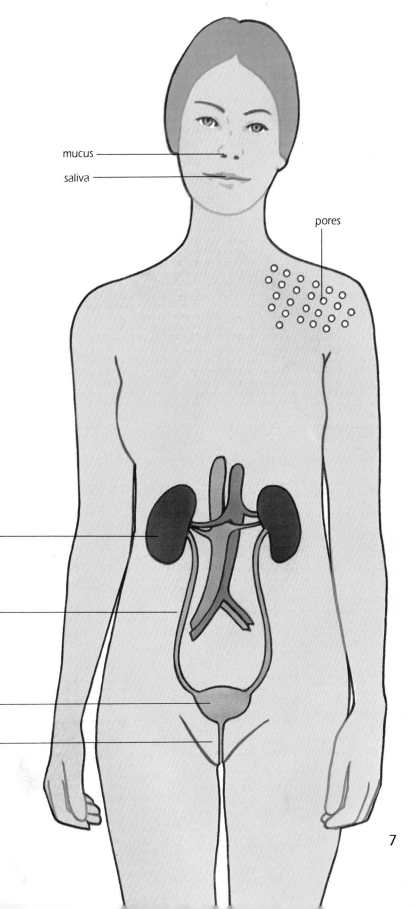

mucus

saliva

pores

kidneys

ureter

bladder

urethra

Water for plants

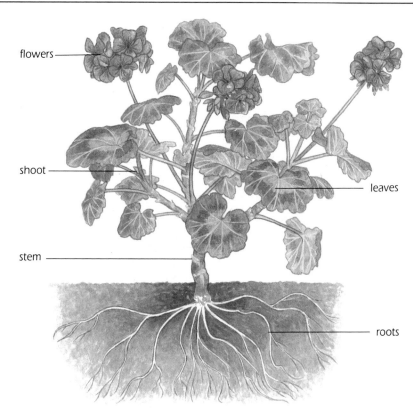

flowers

shoot

stem

leaves

roots

▶ Plants take water in through their roots. The water is then transferred along tubes to the stems, shoots, leaves, and flowers. The plant gets rid of water through tiny holes in its leaves called stomata. Stomata are like the pores we have in our skin.

Plants need water just as much as people and animals. Watch what happens if you grow two plants in separate pots but in the same type of soil. If one gets water every day, it will grow well. If the other is not given any water at all, it will die. Watering plants like this is called **irrigation**. You use irrigation if you water plants with a watering can or if you wet the lawn with a hose or sprinkler.

Through the roots

The plants we grow outside for food get most of the water they need from the rain. These crops need extra water from irrigation when it is too dry for many days at a time. This happens in many parts of the world, not just in the hot, dry lands. Plants take up the water they need through their roots. This

is why the roots are often long and why they spread out under the soil. The way in which they soak up water from the soil and into their roots is called **osmosis**.

Water in dry lands

Irrigation is used a lot in hot, dry lands. There, the weather is hot enough to grow crops, but not wet enough to give the crops the water they need. Farmers make up for this by taking some water from rivers or wells. They use machines, such as a wooden crane called a **shadoof**, to lift the water out of the river. The water is emptied into an irrigation ditch. It flows along the ditch to the fields. This is not always a reliable way to grow crops since many rivers dry up just at the time when water is most needed.

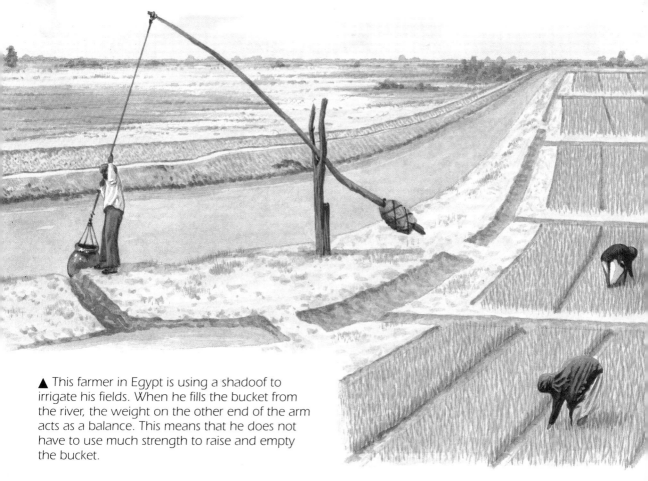

▲ This farmer in Egypt is using a shadoof to irrigate his fields. When he fills the bucket from the river, the weight on the other end of the arm acts as a balance. This means that he does not have to use much strength to raise and empty the bucket.

Storing water

A better way is to store water in a lake built specially for use in the dry weather. First, dams are built across rivers. The dam holds back the water carried by the river in the rainy season. Then the lake, or **reservoir**, which forms behind the walls of the dam is still full of water when the dry season starts.

Pipes or irrigation ditches take the water to the fields. Building dams can help to solve many of the problems of dry lands where people starve when their crops do not grow.

▶ Some crops, such as rice, can only grow well when water completely covers the ground. These paddy fields are flooded by the tropical, or monsoon rains. The rice crop is planted in the flooded fields. The plants grow in water until they are ready for harvesting. Then the fields are drained.

Water for towns

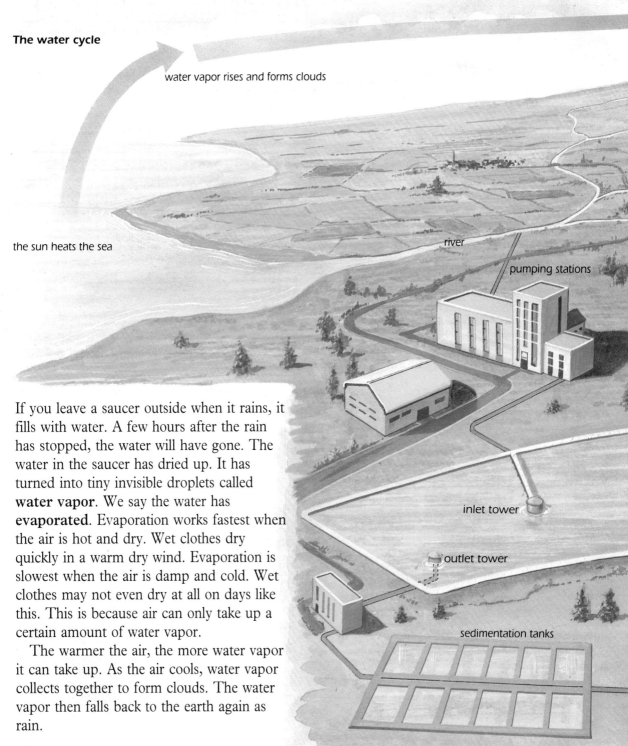

The water cycle

water vapor rises and forms clouds

the sun heats the sea

river

pumping stations

inlet tower

outlet tower

sedimentation tanks

If you leave a saucer outside when it rains, it fills with water. A few hours after the rain has stopped, the water will have gone. The water in the saucer has dried up. It has turned into tiny invisible droplets called **water vapor**. We say the water has **evaporated**. Evaporation works fastest when the air is hot and dry. Wet clothes dry quickly in a warm dry wind. Evaporation is slowest when the air is damp and cold. Wet clothes may not even dry at all on days like this. This is because air can only take up a certain amount of water vapor.

The warmer the air, the more water vapor it can take up. As the air cools, water vapor collects together to form clouds. The water vapor then falls back to the earth again as rain.

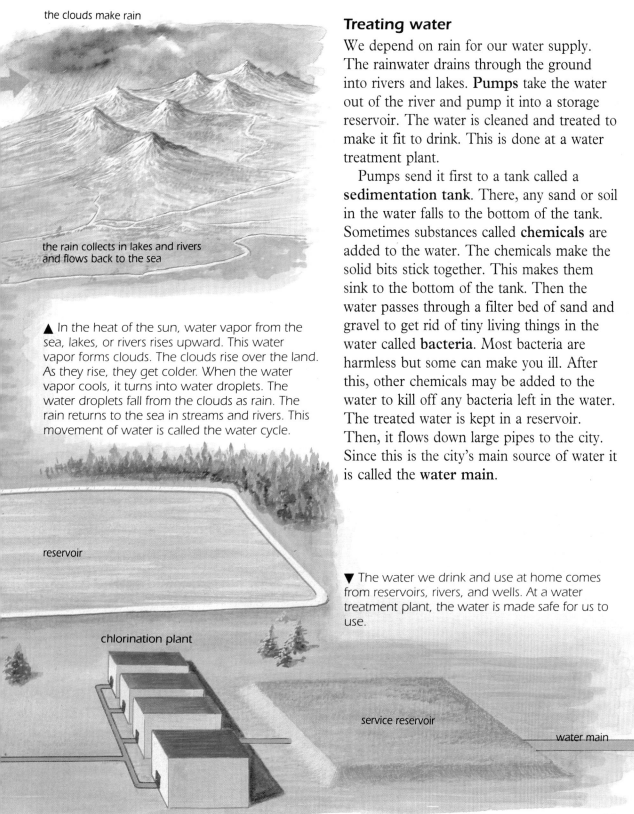

the clouds make rain

the rain collects in lakes and rivers
and flows back to the sea

▲ In the heat of the sun, water vapor from the sea, lakes, or rivers rises upward. This water vapor forms clouds. The clouds rise over the land. As they rise, they get colder. When the water vapor cools, it turns into water droplets. The water droplets fall from the clouds as rain. The rain returns to the sea in streams and rivers. This movement of water is called the water cycle.

reservoir

chlorination plant

service reservoir

water main

Treating water

We depend on rain for our water supply. The rainwater drains through the ground into rivers and lakes. **Pumps** take the water out of the river and pump it into a storage reservoir. The water is cleaned and treated to make it fit to drink. This is done at a water treatment plant.

Pumps send it first to a tank called a **sedimentation tank**. There, any sand or soil in the water falls to the bottom of the tank. Sometimes substances called **chemicals** are added to the water. The chemicals make the solid bits stick together. This makes them sink to the bottom of the tank. Then the water passes through a filter bed of sand and gravel to get rid of tiny living things in the water called **bacteria**. Most bacteria are harmless but some can make you ill. After this, other chemicals may be added to the water to kill off any bacteria left in the water. The treated water is kept in a reservoir. Then, it flows down large pipes to the city. Since this is the city's main source of water it is called the **water main**.

▼ The water we drink and use at home comes from reservoirs, rivers, and wells. At a water treatment plant, the water is made safe for us to use.

11

Water in the home

The water you use at home comes from the water main pipe in the road or street outside. A smaller pipe brings water from the main into your home. The supply of this water is regulated by a **control valve**. If you open the **valve** the water flows along the pipe into the house. If you need to repair a leaking pipe, you can turn the water off at the control valve.

Water in the home

The pipe carrying the water into your home is called the water main. It supplies clean drinking water. The water may go straight to the taps or, in some places, it may go to a water storage tank on the roof. In some houses the water then flows down the pipes to all the cold water taps or the water heaters. It does not have to be pumped.

▶ The water system in your home may be like this one. Some houses have a water storage tank that holds the water in the house. In other houses, all the water is supplied directly from the city's water main.

▼ The hot water may be heated in the hot water tank or may come from the boiler in the central heating system.

▶ The bend in the water main pipe is called a gooseneck. When the weather gets very hot, the pipe gets bigger. When the weather gets colder, it gets smaller. The gooseneck lets the pipe get bigger and smaller without affecting the water main pipe or the pipes inside the building.

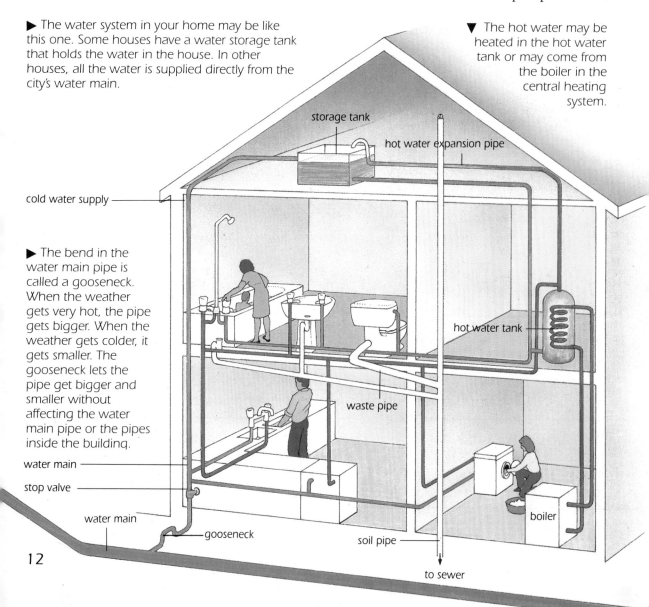

storage tank

hot water expansion pipe

cold water supply

hot water tank

waste pipe

water main

stop valve

water main

gooseneck

soil pipe

boiler

to sewer

How a faucet works

When you turn on a faucet you are really turning a screw. As you turn the handle on, the screw lets go of a **washer** beneath the handle. This opens a gap that lets water in the pipe flow through. When you tighten the handle again, the screw pushes down on the washer to stop water from getting past. The washer makes the faucet watertight. Washers often wear away after a time and allow the faucet to leak.

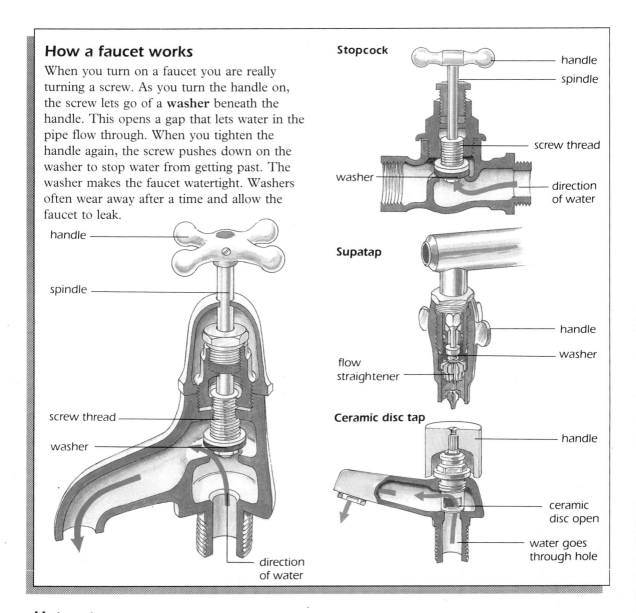

handle

spindle

screw thread

washer

direction of water

Stopcock

handle

spindle

screw thread

washer

direction of water

Supatap

handle

washer

flow straightener

Ceramic disc tap

handle

ceramic disc open

water goes through hole

Hot water

Most homes store hot water in a tank. The cold water may go into the hot water tank through a pipe at the bottom. Then it is made hot by an electrically heated rod called a **heating element**. Water, like air, rises when it is hot and sinks when it is cold. The water in the hot water tank is always hotter at the top than it is at the bottom. If the water is heated by the central heating system it may come from the **boiler**. The boiler is some distance from the tank. The hot water from the boiler rises up a pipe called the supply pipe. The hot water then goes into the hottest part of the hot water tank at the top. The hot water flows from this tank into pipes which take it to all the hot taps in the building. If the water in the hot water tank gets too hot, it rises up a pipe called the expansion pipe. The hot water then spills over into the tank in the roof space.

13

Hot baths

The Romans, who lived about 2,000 years ago, used a lot of water. Having a good water supply was very important to them. They built baths in their biggest cities and in the homes of many rich people. At the baths some rooms were hot and steamy and other rooms were hot and dry. Baths like this were also used in the Arab world during the Middle Ages. Today, having a **sauna** is not much different from having a bath in Roman times.

Taking a shower

Many people think that taking a shower is a better way to use hot water to wash ourselves than taking a bath. A shower uses less water. It also rinses the dirty, soapy water away. The water from the shower makes a fine spray because it comes from a ring of tiny holes in the shower **nozzle**. The nozzle forces the flow of water through the tiny holes to make a spray. The temperature of

◀ The air inside a sauna is very hot and very dry. It makes the bathers hot. They sweat a lot. Then they plunge into cold water or have a cold shower to cool down.

the water is controlled by the shower valves. The valves allow hot water from the hot pipe to mix with cold water from the cold pipe to make the water warm enough to use. You can decide how warm you want the water to be by adjusting the control valves. Once, you had to take great care when you had a shower. If someone in another apartment turned on the water at the same time, it sometimes reduced the amount of water coming through the nozzle. Suddenly the water in the shower could turn very hot instead of warm! Now most showers have a control which cuts off the water supply if the cold water gets too low.

▼ Hot baths can make you feel warm and relaxed. Showers often make you feel fresh and lively. Some modern baths called Jacuzzis have jets of water which make the water bubble and froth like a whirlpool. It is like having a shower and a bath at the same time!

Taking a shower

The temperature of the water heater is controlled by a **thermostat**. The thermostat stops the water from getting too hot or too cold. When you set the dial, this tells the thermostat how hot you want the water to be. The thermostat measures the temperature of the water in the tank. If the temperature is too hot, you cut down the amount of hot water coming into the shower with the control valves. You can also let in more cold water. If the water is too cold, then more hot water is added.

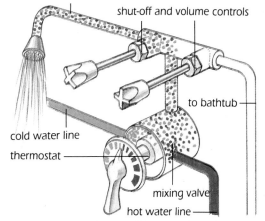

to shower

shut-off and volume controls

to bathtub

cold water line

thermostat

mixing valve

hot water line

Getting rid of waste

We need a good water supply to keep us clean and healthy. We need water for washing our bodies and our clothes, and for washing away our waste. In many parts of the world one of the main uses of water in the home is to flush the toilet. Water is used for several important reasons. Our waste carries a lot of bacteria in it. If these are not washed away they can make us very ill. Adding a lot of water to a harmful or unpleasant liquid dilutes it and makes it less harmful. Fast running water can be used to break up solids and force them down narrow pipes. It also keeps the pipes clean and stops them from getting blocked.

A ball-float

The tank at the top of the toilet is filled with cold water. When you push the handle down, this water empties into the toilet bowl below. The clean water pushes the contents of the bowl down into a pipe that leads outside. This is called the soil pipe. The soil pipe then empties the contents into a drain or **sewer** under the ground.

The toilet flushes because the handle you push is joined to a lever inside the tank. This lever lifts a plunger connected to a valve seat which lets the water rush into the toilet bowl. At the same time, more water comes in to fill up the tank, through an inlet pipe.

When the tank is full, the supply of new water is shut off automatically. This is done with a float ball. This is a hollow ball attached to a rod. When the water empties out of the tank and into the bowl, the float ball drops to the bottom of the tank. As the tank refills, the water level rises and the float

▲ It was about 200 years ago that the flush toilet was invented. It was called a water closet. The tank was high up near the ceiling like this one. The water fell from a height, like a waterfall, to clean the pan.

ball moves up with the water. When the float ball reaches the top of the tank, the end of the rod to which it is attached shuts off the supply of water.

If this didn't happen the water would continue to flow. It would not flood the floor, however. The extra water would simply run out through a pipe in the tank, called an **overflow pipe**.

16

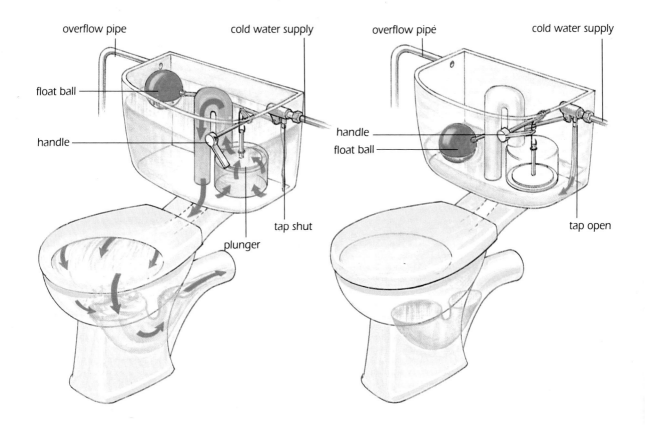

overflow pipe

cold water supply

float ball

handle

tap shut

plunger

overflow pipe

cold water supply

handle

float ball

tap open

▲ What happens when you flush the toilet.

When you press the handle, the plunger releases the water into the toilet bowl. The tank automatically refills with water.

▲ The float ball goes down with the water level and the arm pulls open the valve on the inlet pipe. The rising water lifts the float ball and when the water level is high enough the lever shuts off the valve again.

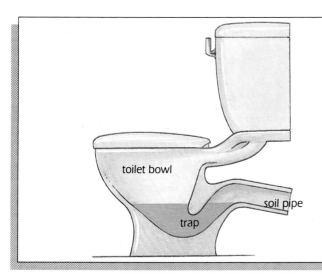

toilet bowl

soil pipe

trap

Stopping smells

You may have noticed there is always water at the bottom of a toilet bowl. This is because the pipe below the pan has a large bend in it, called the **trap**. This traps the last of the new water each time the toilet flushes. The water is like a wall. It stops smells coming back into the house from the soil pipe.

Down the drain

The water from a toilet goes into the main drain pipe or sewer under the ground. Each sink, bath, and shower in the home also has a drain that empties the water into a main drain pipe. Other pipes catch rainwater as it drains off roofs. All this water finds its way into the huge pipes or tunnels which lie below the streets of our cities. These are the sewer mains.

▼ Some workers maintain the sewers of a city. They repair the lining of the tunnels and sort out problems if there is flooding or blockage.

Under the city

The liquid waste or sewage from all the buildings in the city flows through these sewers. It is carried along by running water. The sewers connect with each other to form a large maze of tunnels underground. In big cities they are often lined with bricks or concrete. They may be high enough to let workers walk through them upright. During a heavy rainfall, the tunnels fill up with floodwater and the sewage flows along in swirling streams. In places it even forms waterfalls where there are steep drops in the tunnels.

Rotting sewage

The main sewer carries the waste to a sewage treatment plant. This is an area of land with large tanks. There, the sewage is quickly broken down and made harmless. If the sewage was left in the open air it would rot. This is because the bacteria in the sewage reacts with the **oxygen** in the air to break up the sewage. Rotting also makes sewage harmless, but it is unpleasant to see and smell.

At a sewage treatmentplant

The sewage is first piped into tanks. The solid waste sinks to the bottom to form **sludge**.

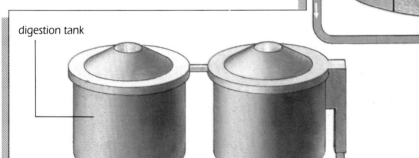

sewage

sedimentation tanks

sludge

liquid sewage

digestion tank

Oxygen is added to the sludge. The oxygen reacts with the bacteria to make the sludge harmless.

aeration tanks

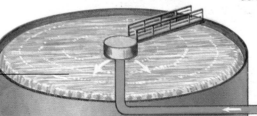

filter beds

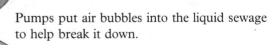

Pumps put air bubbles into the liquid sewage to help break it down.

The liquid trickles slowly through the sand and gravel. Any remaining waste products are trapped.

Clean water flows out. A chemical called **chlorine** is added to the water. The chlorine kills any remaining germs.

Washing clothes

Washing clothes is a major use of water. In some places in the world clothes are washed in rivers or lakes. It is easier to clean clothes with hot water than with cold water. Washing machines in homes use water and electricity to wash clothes.

Many people use **automatic** washing machines to wash their clothes. When you set the washer dials, a **program** tells the washing machine what actions to perform and what water temperature or temperatures to use.

The washing cycle

1 Cold, warm, or hot water comes into the machine through the inlet hose. A valve closes off the inlet hose when the machine has been filled.

3 The drain hose takes the dirty water away to the drain

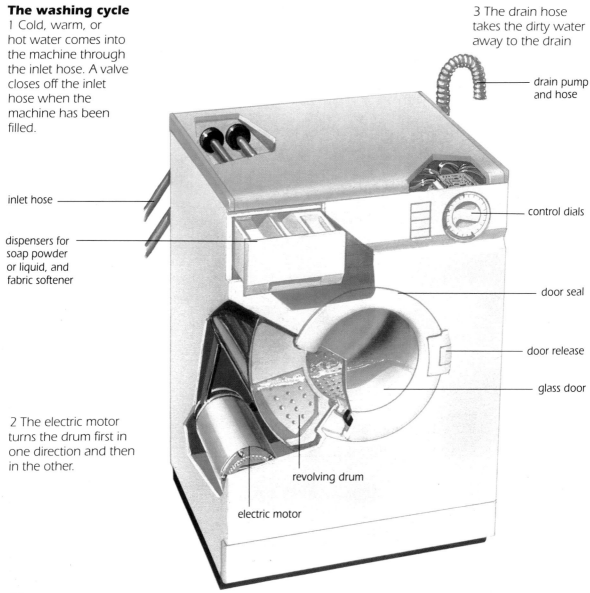

drain pump and hose

inlet hose

dispensers for soap powder or liquid, and fabric softener

control dials

door seal

door release

glass door

2 The electric motor turns the drum first in one direction and then in the other.

revolving drum

electric motor

In the wash

The dirty clothes are first put into a round drum inside the washing machine. A motor makes the drum move. Springs hold the drum in place and stop it from shaking. Small metal balls, called ball bearings, help to make the drum spin around smoothly at high speed. The program tells the machine when to take water in from an inlet pipe. The thermostat also controls the temperature of the water and the length of the wash, rinse, and spin cycles.

The clothes are washed with a special washing powder or liquid. This helps to break down the dirt in the clothes. In most machines the electric motor turns the drum first in one direction and then in the other. This spreads the water and detergent through all the clothes. The movement also helps to remove the dirt broken down by the washing powder.

Rinsing clothes

When the clothes have been washed the dirty water empties out and clean water takes its place. A drain hose takes away the dirty water to the drains outside. The clean water rinses the clothes to get rid of any of the washing powder and loose dirt that may be clinging to the clothes. There may be several rinses before the rinse cycle is finished.

Finally, the water is drained away and the electric motor spins the drum around at high speed to remove any excess water from the clothes.

▲ This washing machine is over a hundred years old. The first washing machines were very simple. The clothes were boiled in a tank of water, stirred with a rod and later squeezed through rollers to get rid of the water.

Spinning the clothes

As the drum spins, water is forced out of the clothes. Because the drum spins or rotates very quickly, the clothes are squeezed tight against the sides of the drum as it goes around and around. This is called spin drying. Holes in the surface of the drum let the surplus water flow out to the drain.

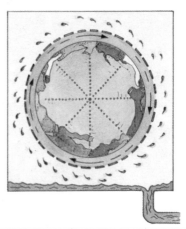

21

Washing dishes

People also use water to wash dirty dishes, pots, and pans. Hot water is used because it melts the grease and fats stuck to the plates and dishes. The hot water helps to dissolve substances such as salt and sugar. Hot water also softens other foods that may be stuck to the plates. However, when pots and pans are washed by hand in a sink, the water is usually warm rather than hot. This is because temperatures of more than 148°F (50°C) are too hot for most people's hands.

▶ A person washing dishes can spend as much as 500 hours a year at the sink. Washing plates and dishes by hand has many drawbacks. The water slowly gets dirtier. The dishes are not always rinsed clean in fresh hot water. Using a towel to dry them may even put dirt back on to the surface of the plates and dishes.

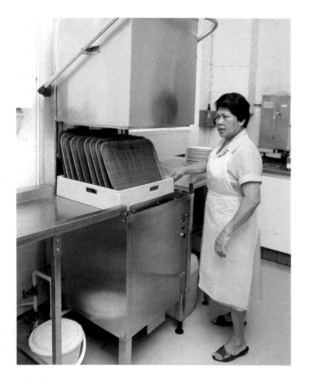

Washing by machine

An automatic dishwasher heats water to temperatures of between 166°F (60°C) and 184°F (70°C). This is why a dishwasher is very good at removing dirt and grease. It also helps to get rid of bacteria in the dirt that might spread diseases and infections. The bacteria cannot survive when very hot water is sprayed onto the dishes. The dishwasher uses a cleaning powder to break down the food left on the plates.

◀ This commercial dishwasher is being used in a hospital. It needs to be able to wash thousands of dirty plates, cups, and trays every day. Dishwashers like this have to be strong because they are working all the time. They also have to work much faster than dishwashers in the home.

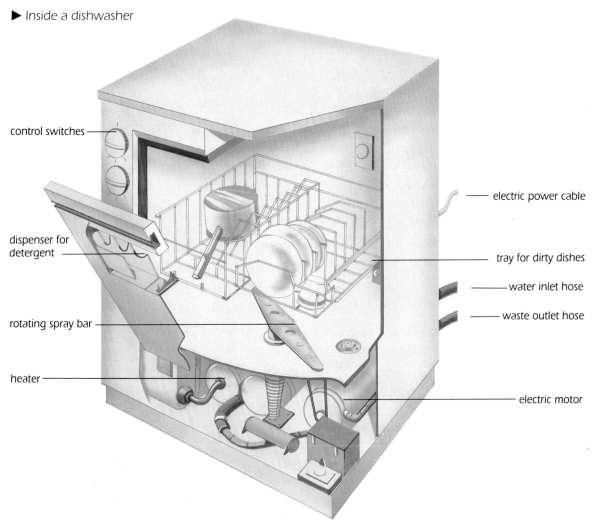

▶ Inside a dishwasher

control switches

electric power cable

dispenser for detergent

tray for dirty dishes

water inlet hose

waste outlet hose

rotating spray bar

heater

electric motor

Washing with sprays

The pots, glasses, pans, and silverware are stacked inside the dishwasher on racks. The water enters the machine through the inlet hose. The amount of water is regulated by a control valve. Some dishwashers use cold water at first to soften the food on the plates. Using very hot water at the start might bake the grease onto the dishes and make them harder to clean.

An electric heating element controlled by a thermostat heats the water. Electricity also turns revolving arms that sprays hot water onto the dishes. These arms are connected to the electric motor by rubber belts, called **drive belts**. This is at the bottom of the dishwasher. Pumps push hot water out through the spray holes in the arms. These high-powered jets of hot water contain cleaning powder and strip the dirt from the dishes. The dirt that has been washed off the dishes is trapped in **filters**. After the dishes have been washed, clean hot water is pumped through the revolving arms to rinse the dishes clean.

Heating with water

Do you have central heating in your home? If you do, the heat may come from electricity or from gas, oil, or coal burned in a boiler. This heat may be taken around the house as steam.

The first hot water central heating system was invented in France about 200 years ago. This system used a group of large, metal pipes filled with water. When the water was heated, the surface of the pipes became hot. Some of this heat passed out or **radiated** from the pipes into the room. Most of the heat warmed the air next to the pipes. This warm air then moved around the room. The pipes were called radiators. Today, the pipes of a radiator are usually in nests of tubes.

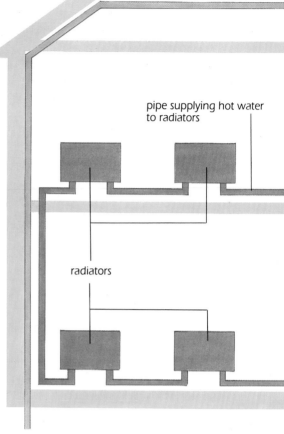

pipe supplying hot water to radiators

radiators

▲ Central heating with water. Only a small amount of water is needed to fill the radiators in a central heating system. The water moves around the system continuously, returning to the boiler to be reheated.

Controlling central heating

A **timer** and a thermostat are used to control the central heating system. The timer looks like a clock. You turn the dial to set the central heating to switch on and off at fixed times of the day. The thermostat is put inside one of the rooms. It switches the boiler on if the temperature of the air in the room falls below the level set on the dial. The thermostat turns the boiler off again when the air is warm enough.

Heating through pipes

Central heating systems that use water get their heat from a **boiler**. The boiler burns a fuel, such as oil, gas, or coal, or uses electricity. The water is heated to the temperature set by the boiler's thermostat. Pumps send the hot water through pipes and these feed hot water into the radiators. The central heating system works because the hot water in each radiator heats the whole of the

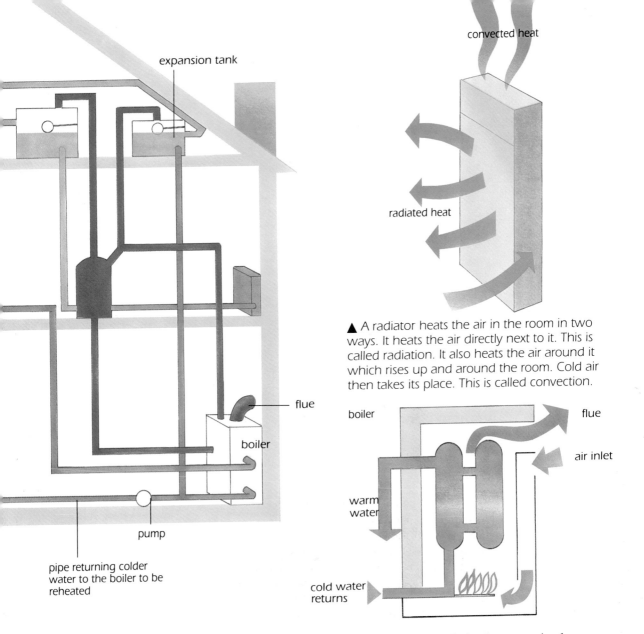

expansion tank

convected heat

radiated heat

▲ A radiator heats the air in the room in two ways. It heats the air directly next to it. This is called radiation. It also heats the air around it which rises up and around the room. Cold air then takes its place. This is called convection.

flue

boiler

pump

pipe returning colder water to the boiler to be reheated

boiler

flue

air inlet

warm water

cold water returns

surface of the radiator. The heat passes from the hot water into the metal surface. We call the way this heat moves **conduction**. In turn, the radiator sends this heat into the room in two main ways. First, it radiates some heat directly into the room. You can feel this warmth on your face if you sit near the radiator. Second, the radiator heats the air around it. This warmed air rises and colder air moves in below it to take its place.

This means the air in the room is always moving in a circle. This is called **convection** heating.

The heat lost from the radiators must be replaced, otherwise the radiators will get cold. This is why the pump sends the water back to the boiler to be reheated. In this way hot water is always moving through the radiators.

Cooling with water

Water is an amazing liquid. Not only can it be used for heating, it can also be used for cooling. When you are hot, you can cool off with an iced drink or a swim.

Water also cools machines. Water in a car radiator is used to cool the engine down. The engine heats up because the moving parts rub against each other. As they do this they get hotter and hotter. We say they are making **friction**. Friction makes heat. If the water in the car engine did not cool the moving parts down, they would be damaged and the engine would lock up.

Cooling a car engine

The cool water at the bottom of the radiator is pumped through a rubber hose to the engine. Heat from the engine passes into this water and the engine cools down. The hot water from the engine returns to the top of the radiator through another rubber hose. The water then cools as it falls through the long, thin pipes in the radiator. The tiny gaps in the radiator let cold air pass through as the car is driven. The moving air cools the water.

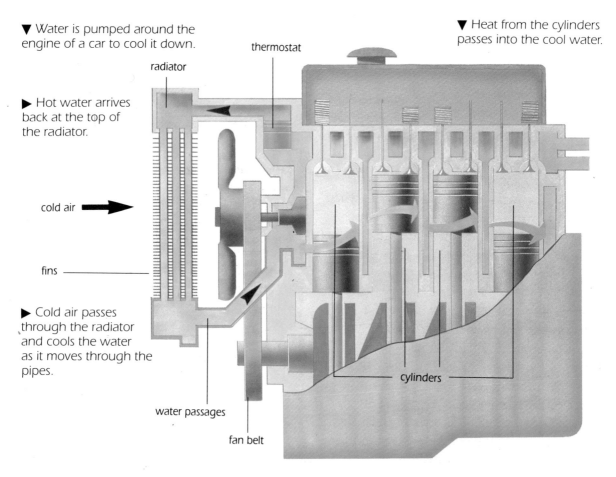

▼ Water is pumped around the engine of a car to cool it down.

thermostat

radiator

▶ Hot water arrives back at the top of the radiator.

cold air ➡

fins

▶ Cold air passes through the radiator and cools the water as it moves through the pipes.

water passages

fan belt

▼ Heat from the cylinders passes into the cool water.

cylinders

► If the water in a car radiator gets too hot, it turns to steam. The driver sees clouds of steam coming from the hood. This sometimes happens when a car has to be driven slowly for a long time in traffic, especially if the car is old. However, usually this rise in heat shows on the temperature gauge to warn the driver before the water starts to boil.

A **fan** spins around in front of the radiator. The fan also helps to draw in air from outside. This helps cool the water when the car is standing still or moving slowly. The cooled water returns to the engine through the hose at the bottom. It is used over and over again.

Stopping ice

There is one big problem with using water to cool a car engine. Water freezes if its temperature falls below 32°F (0°C). When water freezes it gets bigger. It expands. If the water around the cylinders freezes, the ice will crack the engine. To stop this happening, we mix the water in car radiators with a chemical called **antifreeze**.

How anti freeze works

Antifreeze lowers the freezing point of water in a car's cooling system. If we add one part of antifreeze to three parts of water, ice will not form until the temperature falls below -25°F (-18°C). If we add more antifreeze, the ice will not form at even lower temperatures.

one part anti freeze

three parts water

Putting out a fire

If a big fire broke out long ago there was little that people could do. They could put out small fires with buckets of water. But most houses were made of wood and had straw roofs. They burned quickly. People could not get close enough to throw water on the flames. Most of the world's large towns and cities had great fires at one time in their past. The Great Fire of London was in 1666. After the fire the streets were so hot that people couldn't walk in them for three days. In 1871 Chicago had a great fire which burned down nearly 20,000 homes. Water was used to try to put out these fires. It had to be carried from rivers and streams in buckets or small carts.

▼ These fire fighters are using high-pressure hoses to put out the fire. When a large amount of water is forced through a small pipe, it comes out as a very powerful stream. This means it will reach a long way. It often takes two fire fighters to hold each hose steady.

Fire fighters

Now most countries train special teams of people to put out fires. These fire fighters have to be ready at a moment's notice to go to the scene of a fire. Water still plays a big part in their work. They use fire engines fitted with hoses and strong pumps that can send powerful jets of water into the sky. A fire engine can pump out water at a rate of over 1,000 gallons (4,000 liters) a minute.

The fire engine draws the water from special faucets, called **fire hydrants**. These are part of the water supply that flows under the streets. A fire engine can also use water pumped out from a river, lake, or even from a farm pond to attack the flames. Water is the main weapon in the fight against fire. It cools the fire down, since the heat alone can make things burst into flames. It also helps to smother the fire, cutting off the air the fire needs to keep burning. At the same time it soaks materials nearby. This is important because wet things take longer to catch fire.

◀ This plate shows the location of a fire hydrant under the ground in Britain.

▲ Fire hydrants in New York are above ground. Although it is illegal to do so, children use the water to cool off in the summer.

How water stops fire

Water helps to put out fires in two ways. Wet things do not burn so easily. Also, water helps to cut off the air from the fire, and flames need oxygen from air to keep burning. Today we sometimes use foam instead of water to cut off oxygen from a fire.

Using steam

When water is poured onto a fire some of it turns into steam. Steam is water vapor that comes from boiling water. Water turns to steam when it is heated to a temperature of 212°F (100°C). In some ways steam is more useful than water. As the water turns into steam it expands. It can expand about 1,700 times. Unlike water, it can be squeezed, or **compressed,** into a smaller space.

Steam is also useful because it is hotter than water. Steam is hot enough to kill bacteria. They cannot live in such heat. This is why hospitals use steam to clean the instruments used in an operation. Scalding the instruments with steam, or **sterilizing** them, leaves them free from bacteria.

In the kitchen

Cooks use steam in the kitchen to cook many foods. Some foods, such as fish, are easily cooked by the movement of steam from boiling water. The fish is put in a container with small holes in the bottom. The container rests on top of a pan of boiling water. Steam from the pan passes through the holes in the container and heats the fish without boiling it. The Chinese use steamers to cook much of their food as the food is cooked very quickly and remains crisp.

▼ Vegetables are being cooked by steam in this steamer. The steam stops them from drying out. Vegetables cooked by steam keep more of their vitamins than vegetables cooked in water. Vitamins in food help keep us healthy.

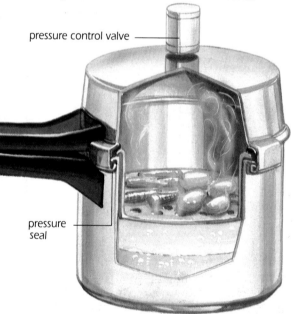

pressure control valve

pressure seal

▲ Pressure cookers use valves to keep the steam safely under pressure. When the steam reaches the correct pressure, some of it escapes through the valve. The valve keeps the pressure in the cooker constant.

holes

steam

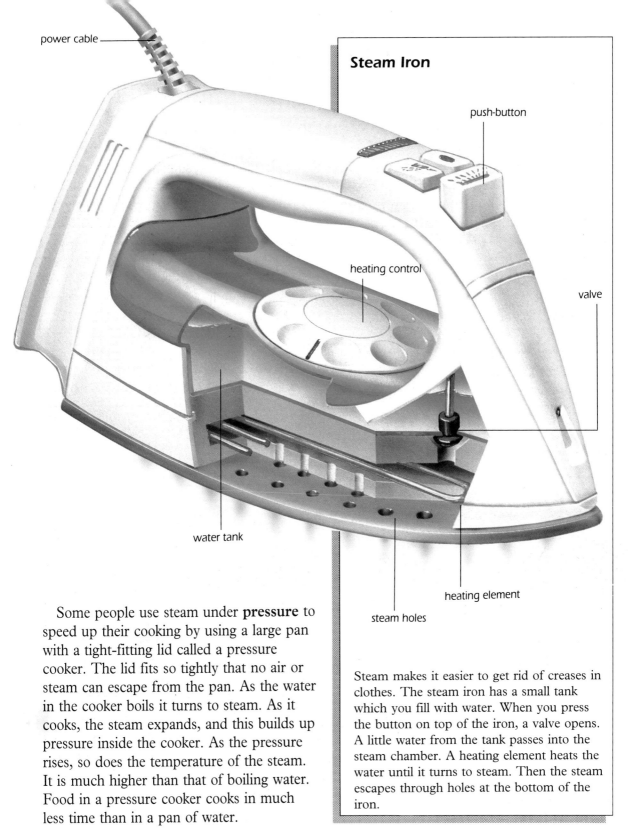

power cable

Steam Iron

push-button

heating control

valve

water tank

heating element

steam holes

Some people use steam under **pressure** to speed up their cooking by using a large pan with a tight-fitting lid called a pressure cooker. The lid fits so tightly that no air or steam can escape from the pan. As the water in the cooker boils it turns to steam. As it cooks, the steam expands, and this builds up pressure inside the cooker. As the pressure rises, so does the temperature of the steam. It is much higher than that of boiling water. Food in a pressure cooker cooks in much less time than in a pan of water.

Steam makes it easier to get rid of creases in clothes. The steam iron has a small tank which you fill with water. When you press the button on top of the iron, a valve opens. A little water from the tank passes into the steam chamber. A heating element heats the water until it turns to steam. Then the steam escapes through holes at the bottom of the iron.

Steam power

Steam kept under pressure is very powerful. It is a source of energy. This is why in the past it was used to drive machines and vehicles. The first **steam engines** were invented about 300 years ago. In these engines, the pressure of the steam pushed a **piston** up and down a cylinder. At first, this up-and-down motion was just used to pump water out of tin and coal mines. It was not used to drive machines until about 200 years ago. It was then that James Watt found a way of changing the up-and-down movement of the piston to turn wheels.

▼ Steam-powered tractors called traction engines were a common sight in the countryside 100 years ago. These huge tractors had tall smoking chimneys. They were also very noisy and dirty. They worked the threshing machines that separated the ears of wheat from the straw. This old steam engine is on show at a museum.

New machines

Steam engines took over the hard work in the new factories that opened 200 years ago. The engines worked much faster and much more cheaply than workers could by hand. Soon people thought of other ways of using the power in steam. They used it to turn the wheels of **steam locomotives**. They also used it to turn the **paddle wheels** of the first steamboats and to power steam hammers.

Turning wheels

The first steam locomotives were invented nearly 200 years ago. You can see how they work in the diagram. Coal or wood is used as the fuel. It burns in the firebox to make steam in the boiler. This is made up of many long tubes. These also help heat up the steam. The driver uses **safety valves** to

▼ The heat from the burning coal turns the water in the boiler into steam.

▼ The engineer can open a valve to let steam escape through the whistle.

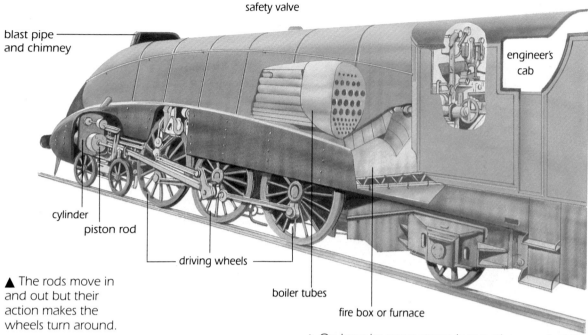

safety valve

blast pipe and chimney

engineer's cab

cylinder

piston rod

driving wheels

▲ The rods move in and out but their action makes the wheels turn around.

boiler tubes

fire box or furnace

▲ On long journeys steam locomotives used a lot of coal and water. This is why they took their fuel and their water with them in the tender, a vehicle that carries a supply of fuel and water behind the engine.

control this steam and keep it under great pressure. They let steam out if the pressure gets too high. Otherwise there might be an explosion. The pressure of the steam from the boiler pushes the pistons in the cylinders below the boiler. In turn, these pistons drive the long rods that turn the wheels.

Steam engines and locomotives made a lot of energy but much of it was wasted. A lot of the steam was lost through the funnel. They used a lot of fuel and were very noisy. The soot from burning the fuel also made everything dirty. Today, we use mostly engines powered by electricity or diesel oil. However, steam locomotives are still used in some parts of the world.

▶ This steam locomotive is in use in India.

The force of water

◄ Hydraulic action has helped to form many of the caves and arches at the coast. Waves crash against the cliffs and force their way into cracks in the rocks.

Unlike gases, liquids cannot be squeezed into smaller spaces. If you press down on a piston in a cylinder of water, the water tries to flow out somewhere else. This happens when you pull the trigger of a squirt gun.

When you exert a force on a piston in a cylinder of water, you increase the pressure in the liquid. Pressure is force per unit area. This pressure is the same everywhere in liquid. If another piston is larger, a larger force is exerted on it. In this way, a small force on a small piston can cause a large force on a large piston.

How hydraulic pressure works

This pipe full of liquid has four outlet pipes which are each the same size as the inlet. When you put a 10-pound weight on the inlet, it creates a pressure that is the same throughout the liquid. The four outlets push out, each with enough pressure to move a 10-pound object. Together they could move a total of 40 pounds.

inlet

four outlets

10   10   10   10   10

equal pressure throughout the liquid

Using water's force

Many machines make use of hydraulic pressure, although most use oil or some other liquid instead of water. This is because water can eat away or corrode metals. Also, since water freezes at 32°F (0°C) it is safer to use a fluid which does not freeze as easily as water.

A forklift truck uses hydraulic pressure. A pump supplies the pressure which forces liquid through tubes on each side of the fork. This lifts the fork and its contents at the front. Service stations use a **hydraulic jack** for lifting a car to change a tire.

The same type of pressure also works the hydraulic brakes in a car. The pressure of a foot on the brake pedal exerts pressure on **brake fluid** in the brake lines to make all four brakes press equally hard at the same time.

▲ Hydraulic lifts can exert great pressure. A person using a hydraulic car jack can lift a heavy vehicle with ease.

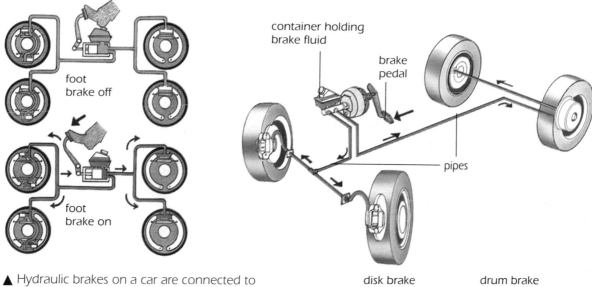

▲ Hydraulic brakes on a car are connected to the brake pedal by tubes, called brake lines. Brake fluid is fed from a central container. When the driver presses the brake pedal the pressure sends the brake fluid through the tubes to all four brakes at once. They all get the same amount of pressure. As a result, they all act together at the same time. The car would swerve if they did not, because one or two brakes would come on before or after the others.

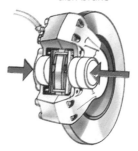

disk brake   drum brake

Water power

The force of flowing water has been used to help people do their work for well over 2,000 years. Large waterwheels were spun around by the movement of rivers. Until steam engines were made, this was the strongest power source for driving machinery. Some waterwheels were sideways, or horizontal, and others were upright, or vertical. As the river flowed along, the water pushed on the wooden boards or blades around the edge of the waterwheel. As the boards were pushed forward, the wheel turned. Rods and **gears** linked the waterwheel to a machine. This was usually a millstone inside a water mill. As the waterwheel turned, so, too, did the millstone. It ground grain to make flour. Much later still, waterwheels were used to turn other machines such as those that spun cotton in the first spinning wheels.

Types of waterwheels

Some waterwheels turned because water from a stream above fell onto buckets on each blade at the top of the wheel. These were **overshot** waterwheels. This type of waterwheel could only be used where there was a waterfall, or where a dam or **weir** had been built across the river. In a **breastshot** waterwheel the water fell on to the edge of the blades where they were level with the middle of the wheel. An **undershot** waterwheel turned because the water pushed the blades at the bottom of the wheel. Undershot waterwheels were often built where the rivers were shallow. They did not move as quickly as overshot wheels.

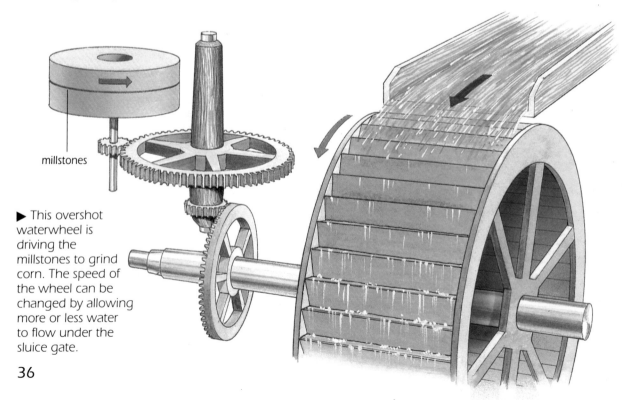

millstones

▶ This overshot waterwheel is driving the millstones to grind corn. The speed of the wheel can be changed by allowing more or less water to flow under the sluice gate.

How waterwheels are used today

The power of a waterwheel or **turbine** is still used today. It is no longer slow moving as it was in the past. The water is made to flow down an upright pipe to the turbine. The pipe is narrower toward the end to make the water push its way through with more force. The powerful jet of water makes the curved blades of the turbine spin around quickly. As the turbine spins around, it drives a machine that makes electricity. Electricity made from water power is called **hydroelectricity**. Turbines used in making hydroelectricity have to be very strong. Their blades are made of metal.

▼ This turbine is part of a hydroelectric plant. The water comes into the turbine with great force and spins the blades.

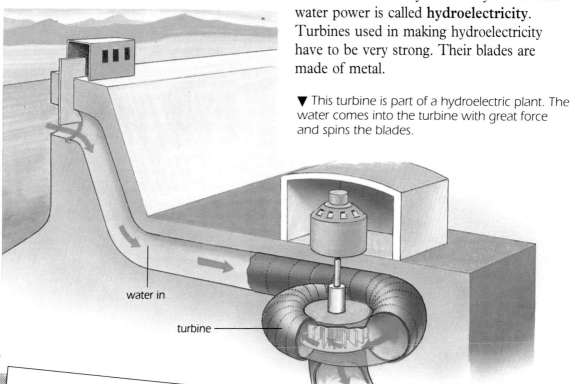

water in

turbine

Wave power

The waves of the sea can cause amazing destruction. For many years scientists have been trying to find a way to turn the power of ocean waves into electricity. There have been small projects all over the world but no one has yet invented a large-scale method of using wave power that is cheap to run.

Electricity from water

Put your hand under a cold water faucet. Feel the force of the water on your hand. Then move your hand down to the bottom of the basin and feel the force of the water again. You should feel a big difference. Now turn the tap on full, so the water flows faster. Can you feel the difference that the extra water makes? The force of the water at a waterfall is the same. It depends on how far it falls and how much water flows. This is called **head water**.

Dams

A good head water at a waterfall can be made to turn a turbine in a hydroelectric power station. The waterfall itself is not used. Instead water is taken from the river

▲ The power of the water at Niagara Falls is very great. These falls power two hydroelectric plants. One is in the United States and the other is in Canada. Each has the capacity to produce nearly 2 million kilowatts of electricity (20 million light bulbs).

above the waterfall. Sometimes a dam is built to hold back the water. The water is channeled into pipes where it falls steeply to the power station below. The water rushes down pipes at a great speed. It hits the turbine blades at the right point to make them spin as fast as possible. The energy made by the turbine is used to power machines called generators. These make electricity. The electricity is sent along wires to towns and cities.

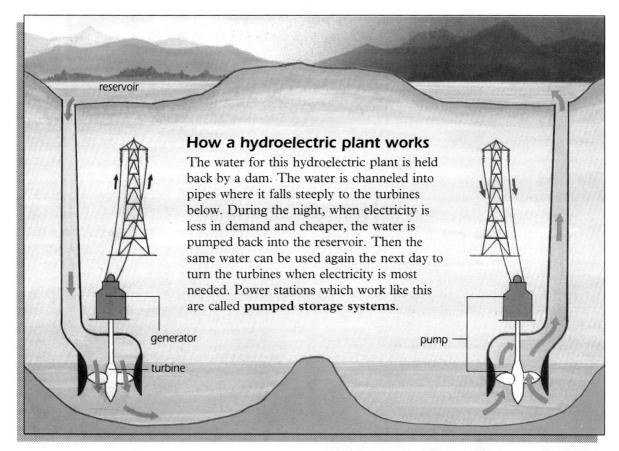

How a hydroelectric plant works

reservoir

The water for this hydroelectric plant is held back by a dam. The water is channeled into pipes where it falls steeply to the turbines below. During the night, when electricity is less in demand and cheaper, the water is pumped back into the reservoir. Then the same water can be used again the next day to turn the turbines when electricity is most needed. Power stations which work like this are called **pumped storage systems**.

generator

turbine

pump

A special type of turbine, called a Pelton turbine, is used for water falling from a great height. This has a series of bucket shaped blades which are spun by a jet of water hitting them. Then the water flows away from underneath.

Using power

Nowadays, over a quarter of the world's electricity comes from hydroelectric power stations. Most have been built among hills and mountains where there are many deep valleys. Dams can be built there to form reservoirs. These areas often have plenty of rain so that the rivers are kept full. Often the best place for a dam may be hundreds of miles from the cities and factories that need the power. The electricity has to be carried by power cables to where it is needed.

▲ The Pelton wheel is used for making electricity from water that falls from a great height.

Water for transportation

Building a hydroelectric dam across a river has one big disadvantage: It makes it impossible for boats and ships to pass. People have used water as a way of traveling for thousands of years. Waterways are still important.

When people first used water for transportation, they traveled in boats on lakes and rivers. Later they went farther afield, sailing on the open sea. Later still, they built waterways called **canals** that could take them across land where there were no natural waterways.

Pushing a boat

It was over 10,000 years ago that Stone Age people found out how to sail across water in a hollowed-out tree trunk. They used the boat for fishing and pushed it through the water using poles. Later people used oars to row boats through water. The oars were like levers. The rower pushed back the water with the oars to move the boat forward.

Then a sail was added so the wind could move the boat. For a long time only a single square sail was used. This only worked when the boat was sailing with the wind.

▼ Paddle steamers had many drawbacks. They used a lot of coal. They were also hard to control in stormy seas. However, they could turn around in a very short space. The wheels looked like waterwheels on each side of the boat.

When the triangular, or lateen, sail was added, the boats could be moved more easily. The lateen sail was fixed so that it could be swung in several directions. A rudder that helped steer the boat was also added. These meant the boats could sail well whichever way the wind was blowing.

About 600 years ago ships became better for traveling across oceans. They had many sails so bigger ships could be moved and they could travel more quickly.

Paddles and propellers

About 200 years ago, the first steamboats were launched. At first, these boats used paddle wheels to push them through the water. About 150 years ago, the **screw propeller** began to take the place of the paddle wheel. It made the boat much easier to control. Screw propellers are used today to push boats of all types from huge ocean liners to small fishing boats.

An outside motor

Many pleasure boats use engines with screw propellers. The engine fits on the outside of the boat. This is why it is called an **outboard motor**. The engine is fixed at the back of the boat above the water. It is usually powered by gasoline. The power from the engine turns a shaft that uses gears to turn the screw propeller, which is under the water. The driver of the powerboat pulls the starter to make the motor turn the propeller. A **throttle** controls the speed of the boat.

▼ The screw propellers on today's large ships are as big as houses. The propeller is under the water at the back of the boat. It is spun around at high speed by the engine. The screw propeller moves the boat through water in the same way as a screwdriver pushes a screw

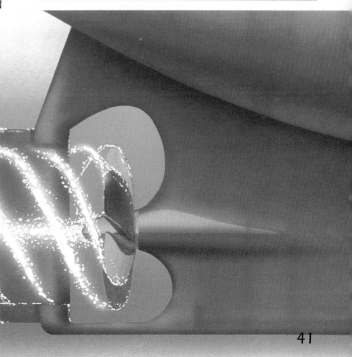

Under the sea

◀ What makes this submarine dive? The ballast tanks have been opened by a control inside the submarine and they are now filling up with sea water. This makes the ship heavier and it sinks. The captain will force the water out of the tanks by pumping air in when the submarine needs to come to the surface again.

You can see how a submarine works if you fill an empty jar with water. Screw the lid on tightly and put the jar in a tub filled with water. The jar sinks to the bottom. Now empty the water out of the jar and put the lid back on. Watch the jar float.

To make a submarine dive below the waves, some water needs to be allowed into the ship. Inside the submarine are large air-filled tanks, called **ballast tanks**, running along both sides of the submarine. When the captain wants the submarine to dive, these tanks are opened up. They fill up with sea water. The submarine is now too heavy to float, so it sinks. The fins on the side of the submarine are tipped to help it to dive below smoothly and quickly.

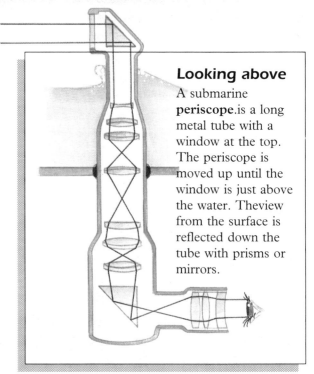

Looking above

A submarine **periscope**.is a long metal tube with a window at the top. The periscope is moved up until the window is just above the water. Theview from the surface is reflected down the tube with prisms or mirrors.

Exploring the sea bed

We tend to think of submarines as war machines, but they have peaceful uses as well. Underwater ships, called **submersibles**, explore the ocean bed. Scientists use submersibles to help them find out more about life at the bottom of the sea.

Moving through the water

When the submarine has reached the level the captain has chosen, a little water is let out of smaller ballast tanks, called trim tanks. The submarine now has just enough water to keep at this level under the water. It also has just enough air to stop it from sinking any further. Valves are used to keep the right amount of air and water in the tanks.

When the captain wants the submarine to return to the surface, compressed air is pumped into the main ballast tanks. The sea water is forced out. This makes the submarine light enough to float once more.

Most submarines are powered by diesel engines. The diesel is used to make electricity, which drives the engines. Some of the electricity is stored in batteries to be used when the submarine is under the sea, since

the diesel engine cannot be used under the sea because it needs air to work. These submarines can only stay at sea for as long as their fuel lasts.

Some submarines use steam to give them power. The heat to make steam is produced in a **nuclear reactor**. This steam drives a turbine that makes electricity and spins the propeller. The steam is then cooled back into water, to be reused. Nuclear-powered submarines can stay underwater for a very long time as they do not need air to drive the motors and they do not need to take on more fuel.

A submarine can sail unseen just below the surface. Yet the captain can see other ships through the ship's periscope. The view from the surface is reflected down the tube with mirrors.

Did you know?

Amazon water

The Amazon River carries so much water to the sea it could fill over two billion quart bottles every second. This would be more than enough water to give every person on the earth as much as they could drink.

Tidal power

A tidal power station was built across the Rance River on the coast of Brittany, France. It opened in 1966. It was the world's first power station to use the tides to make electricity.

Dried food

Dehydrated foods are foods that have had most of the water taken out of them. They occupy far less space than they did before dehydration. Simply by adding water, a single quart of dried milk can be turned into 10 quarts of milk.

Ocean depths

The underwater diving machine, *Trieste*, submerged to a depth of nearly 7 miles in the Pacific Ocean in January 1960.

Deep down

The world's deepest water well is in Montana. It is over one and a half miles deep.

The first submarine

The Italian artist, Leonardo da Vinci, drew plans for a submarine over 450 years ago. It was never built. The first submarine went into action in 1776 during the Revolutionary War.

The water you use

You use at least 150 quarts of water every day. On average, you need about 50 quarts to take a bath or shower. You use another 50 quarts to flush the toilet and a further 50 quarts for drinking, cooking, and washing clothes, dishes, pans, pets, and vehicles.

Warm seas

In future we shall find other ways of using water to help people in their everyday lives. We may even be able to use water itself as a source of energy. Scientists have already tested a method of getting heat from the ocean in tropical seas. The water there is much warmer at the surface than it is deep below. The Ocean Thermal Energy Converter (OTEC) uses the warm sea water on the surface to boil liquids, such as ammonia. Ammonia has a much lower boiling point than water. The gases that are given off spin a turbine to make electricity. Cold water pumped up from deep below the surface cools the used gas. It turns it back into a liquid so the process can begin again.

Glossary

antifreeze: a substance with a low freezing point that is added to water in car radiators to prevent them from freezing and cracking

bacteria: tiny living things that can be found in many places—in the soil, on and in your food, and in your body. Harmful bacteria are called germs.

ballast tanks: large air-filled tanks in a submarine that are filled with water when the submarine needs to submerge

boiler: a container in which water is heated to the boiling point

boiling point: the temperature at which a liquid bubbles and turns into a vapor or gas. Boiling point of water is 212°F (100°C).

brake fluid: a liquid that allows all brakes on a vehicle like a car to work at the same time

breastshot: a waterwheel where the water falls on blades in the middle of the wheel

canals: water channels built across land used by boats

chemicals: substances that can change when joined or mixed with other substances

chlorine: a chemical that is used to kill bacteria in water

compressed: when a substance is reduced in size

conduction: the way in which heat passes between things that are touching

control valve: the valve that regulates the water for your sink, tub, apartment, home, or building

convection: the way in which heat moves through liquids and gases. In convection heating, the hot air rises and the cold air moves in underneath, which means the air is always moving.

crystals: the natural shape of some solids such as salt and sugar

dehydrated: when the water which makes up part of something is removed

drive belts: loops, usually made of rubber, which connect the motors in machines to the parts which need to be moved

energy: the ability to do work. People get energy from food. Engines get energy from fuel like gasoline.

evaporated: when a solid or a liquid is changed into vapor or gas. The gas is often invisible, so we cannot see it in the air.

fan: a device which spins around to produce a current of cool air

filters: devices that remove unwanted solids from liquids

fire hydrants: pipes to which a hose can be attached to obtain water from the water main

freezing point: the temperature at which a liquid freezes and becomes solid. Freezing point of water is 32°F (0°C).

friction: when two surfaces rub together

gas: a substance which is neither liquid nor solid. Air is made up of several gases.

gears: wheels in a machine that create movement when they mesh together

head water: the force of water at a dam or waterfall

heating element: a device that turns electricity into heat

hydraulic jack: a device that uses fluid pressure to raise heavy objects

hydraulic pressure: the pressure in a fluid caused when a force is exerted on a piston

hydroelectricity: electricity that has been made by using fast-flowing water to drive a turbine

hydrogen: a gas that is very light and burns easily. It combines with oxygen to form water.

irrigation: watering the land by using a system of pipes and ditches. The water is pumped from rivers, lakes, or from under the ground. Crops can grow on irrigated land.

kidneys: parts of the body that remove waste matter from the blood. The waste matter is passed into the bladder as urine.

liquid: a substance that is not a solid or a gas. Liquids like water flow.

molecule: a tiny part of a substance that contains all of the qualities found in the substance

mucus: a slimy liquid which people and other animals produce to protect fragile parts of their body, such as the lining of the nose and lungs

nozzle: a small tube. When liquid is pushed through a narrow nozzle, the liquid comes out as a spray.

nuclear reactor: a device that uses nuclear radiation to release heat to boil water to drive steam turbines

osmosis: the way in which plants get water out of the ground

outboard motor: an engine with a screw propeller fitted to the outside of a boat or ship

overflow pipe: a pipe through which spare water flows

overshot: a waterwheel where water is fed from above onto the waterwheel

oxygen: a gas in the air which people, animals, and plants need to stay alive. Fires cannot burn without it.

paddle wheel: the wheel of a steamship or boat that moves it through the water

periscope: a device fitted with mirrors that allows a person below the sea to see objects hidden from the direct line of vision. A submarine captain uses a periscope to look at objects above the sea, when the submarine is submerged below the waves.

piston: a closely fitting rod or disk that moves up and down inside a cylinder

pores: small holes in the skin through which your body can release sweat

pressure: the force exerted on a surface

program: the list of instructions. Automatic washing machines have programs instructing the machine to wash different garments according to their different fabrics.

pump: a machine that sucks gases or liquids through a pipe or tube

pumped storage system: a power station that uses cheap electricity at night to pump the water back into the reservoir so it can be used again

radiate: the way heat goes in straight lines or rays between objects that are not touching

reservoir: a very large tank or lake where water is collected and stored

safety valves: valves that open to allow steam or liquid to escape when pressure is too high

saliva: the watery liquid that your mouth produces to help you eat

sauna: a very hot dry room that makes bathers sweat

screw propeller: a shaft with spiral blades that drives a boat through water

sedimentation tank: a large container in which solid waste sinks to the bottom. The water above it can then be cleaned for reuse.

sewer: a covered drain that carries away solid and liquid waste

shadoof: a machine used to lift water from a river in order to water crops

sludge: wet solids, similar to mud

solid: a substance that is not liquid or gas. It does not flow like water.

solution: a mixture formed by dissolving solids in liquid

steam engine: an engine worked by steam. Steam is a hot gas, formed by boiling a substance like water.

steam locomotive: a railroad engine powered by steam

sterilizing: killing germs using heat or chemicals

submersible: a vessel that can be submerged and travel beneath the surface of the sea

temperature: the measurement of heat or cold

thermostat: a device for controlling temperature

throttle: a valve that controls the supply of gas or steam in a machine

timer: a device on a machine for measuring how much time has passed

trap: a device to stop bad-smelling air escaping from a drain

turbine: a wheel with many curved blades. It is turned by water or a gas. Turbines drive the machines that make electricity.

undershot: a waterwheel driven by water that passes under the wheel

ureter: a tube taking away waste water from the kidneys to the bladder

urethra: a tube taking away the urine from the bladder

valve: a device used to regulate the flow of gases or liquids, generally through a pipe of some kind

washer: a ring put around a tap to make it close tightly

water main: the pipe carrying water into the home from the reservoir

water vapor: water in the form of a gas

weir: a dam in a stream to raise the water level or change its flow

Index